# Life in Space

Originally published as
*Usborne Beginners: Living in Space*

Katie Daynes

Designed by Zoe Wray

Illustrated by Christyan Fox and Alex Pang

Space consultant: Stuart Atkinson

Reading consultant: Alison Kelly,
Roehampton University

## SCHOLASTIC INC.

New York  Toronto  London  Auckland Sydney
Mexico City  New Delhi  Hong Kong  Buenos Aires

# Contents

3   Earth and space

4   Space school

6   Preparing to go

8   Lift off

10  In orbit

12  A home in space

14  The space station

16  Eating and drinking

18  Keeping clean

20  A day in space

22  Spacesuits

24  Going outside

26  Back to Earth

28  Space trips

30  Glossary of space words

31  Web sites to visit

32  Index

# Earth and space

The Earth is a big round planet.
This is what it looks like from space.

Astronauts travel into space to live and work.

The word astronaut means
"star sailor."

# Space school

To become an astronaut, you have to go to space school and learn how to live in space.

On Earth when things jump they go up and then down.

An invisible force called gravity pulls them down.

In space there is very little gravity so everything floats.

Astronauts need lots of training to know what to do when they float in space.

At space school, astronauts learn how to work while floating in water. It feels like working in space.

Astronauts also try out emergency escapes.

They slide down a pole onto a soft mat.

# Preparing to go

Astronauts fly to space in a space shuttle.
The shuttle leaves from a launch pad.

Bridge

The shuttle looks
like a plane
with a big fuel
tank and two
white rockets.

Fuel tank

Launch pad

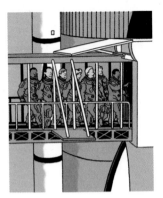

The astronauts put on special orange suits.

They travel to the shuttle in an elevator.

Then they cross a bridge into the shuttle.

The astronauts lie in the nose of the shuttle and wait until it's time to go.

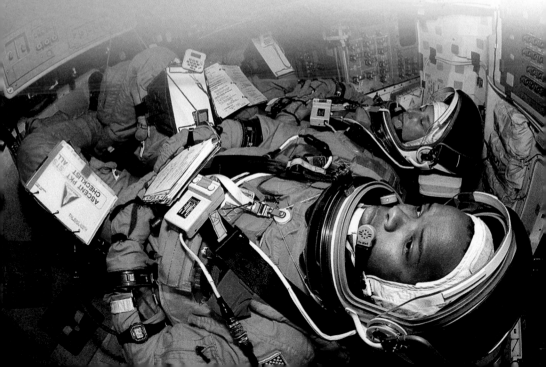

# Lift off

The engines start burning fuel from the fuel tank. Then the two rockets light up and the shuttle zooms into space.

3... 2... 1...
Lift off!

Nobody is allowed to stand close to the launch pad because it is too dangerous.

 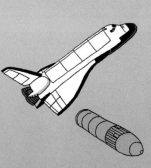 

After two
minutes, the
rockets fall
into the sea.

After eight
minutes, the
fuel tank
falls away.

The shuttle
is now
floating in
space.

Two flaps open up
on the back of the
shuttle so it doesn't
get too hot inside.

# In orbit

The space shuttle goes around the Earth in a big circle. This is known as being in orbit.

It only takes 90 minutes
for the shuttle to
orbit the Earth.

The middle part of the shuttle
is called the payload bay. It
carries big objects into space.

The astronauts work, eat and
sleep in the nose of the shuttle.

# A home in space

Some astronauts stay in space for a long time. They live in a floating home called a space station.

Astronauts are building a big, new space station. This is what it will look like when it's finished.

 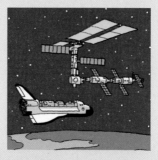 

The shuttle travels through space.

It flies close to the space station.

Then it joins onto the space station.

When the space station is finished, it will be as big as two soccer fields.

# The space station

The space shuttle carries the parts for the new space station into space.

A robot arm on the shuttle picks a big tube out of the payload bay.

The robot arm then joins the new tube onto the space station.

Some of the tubes are as big as a bus.

The astronauts
live in a tube
like this.

Bedroom

Toilet

Shower

Eating area

They wear
everyday clothes
in the space station.

15

# Eating and drinking

When astronauts go into space they take their food and drinks with them.

The first meals taken to space didn't look or taste very nice.

Beef with vegetables

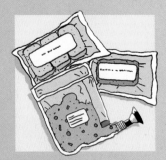

Food was dried and sealed up.

Astronauts added warm water...

...which made the food soggy.

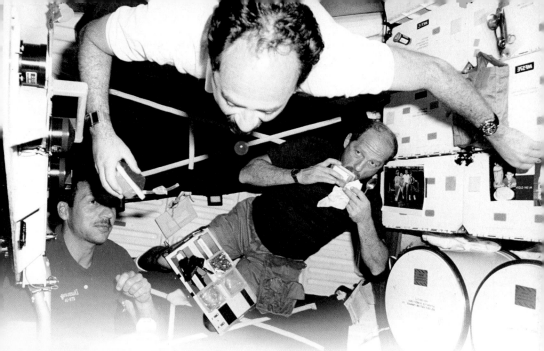

Can you see the blob of drink floating to the astronaut's mouth?

Today, most space meals come already prepared in trays. They just need to be heated. Fruit is dried to keep it fresh.

Dried strawberries

The first man to walk on the Moon ate dried ice cream in space.

# Keeping clean

It is difficult living in a space station. There is not much room and everything floats.

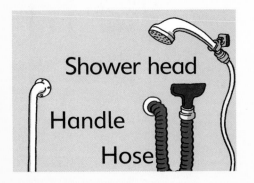

Shower head

Handle

Hose

In a space shower the water flows out then floats in blobs.

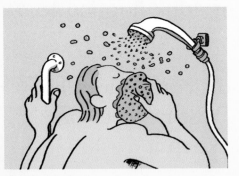

An astronaut holds onto the handle to keep still while he washes.

After rinsing, he uses a hose to suck up all the water.

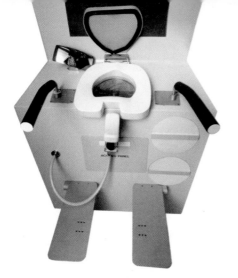

A space toilet has bars and foot rests to help the astronaut sit down.

An astronaut slides the bars over her legs and turns on the air flow.

Astronauts recycle some water in space and more comes from Earth in tanks like these.

# A day in space

Astronauts work in the space station. Some work in a laboratory, like the one below. It's a tube where they can carry out tests.

They also fit new parts inside the space station.

They exercise every day to keep fit and healthy.

They sleep in a sleeping bag attached to the wall.

When they're not working, astronauts read, listen to music, or just look at the amazing views of Earth.

Astronauts can talk to people on Earth and send messages by computer.

# Spacesuits

When astronauts work outside the space station they have to wear a spacesuit.

 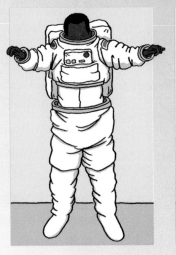 

The first layer keeps them cool or warm.

They add an outer layer for protection.

The helmet and gloves go on last.

Inside their helmets astronauts can drink through a straw and talk to each other.

Straw

A backpack carries air to breathe and water to warm or cool the astronaut.

Space boots aren't made for walking. The astronauts move around by holding onto things with their hands.

# Going outside

Astronauts go out into space through an airlock. It stops air from escaping from the space station.

  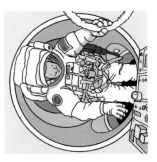

An astronaut goes through the first door.

In the airlock he puts on a spacesuit.

He leaves through the second door.

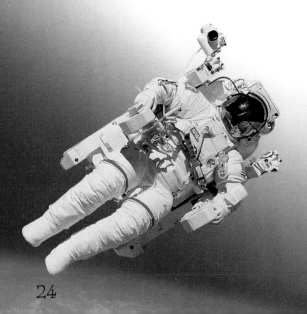

An astronaut sometimes puts on a jet pack so he can move around outside the space station.

When astronauts work outside it is called spacewalking. This astronaut is spacewalking in the shuttle's payload bay.

One astronaut dropped a glove in space. It is still floating around somewhere.

# Back to Earth

After 90 days on the space station the astronauts travel back to Earth.

The shuttle leaves the space station.

It heats up as it drops back through the air.

The shuttle lands on a runway like a plane.

A parachute
helps it to slow down.

The longest an astronaut has stayed
in space is one year and 72 days.

# Space trips

The first trip to space was in 1957.

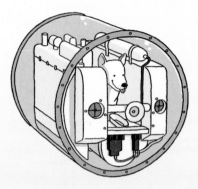

The first living thing to travel from Earth to space was a dog named Laika.

In 1969 astronauts walked on the moon for the first time.

There is no wind or rain on the Moon, so footprints stay for hundreds of years.

In the future you may be able to fly into space in a space plane like this.

People might also live in space homes like this.

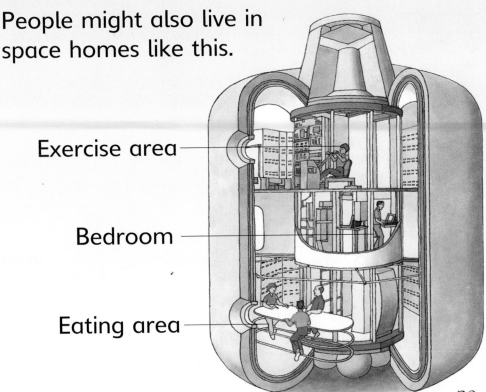

Exercise area

Bedroom

Eating area

# Glossary of space words

Here are some of the words in this book you might not know. This page tells you what they mean.

 planet - a huge round object in space. The Earth is a planet.

 gravity - an invisible force that pulls things on Earth down to the ground.

 fuel - something which burns to give the shuttle power to move very fast.

 in orbit - going around a planet in a big circle.

 payload bay - the middle part of the shuttle where big objects are carried.

 laboratory - a place where people carry out tests.

 airlock - a set of doors for getting into and out of a space station or shuttle.

# Websites to visit

If you have a computer, you can find out more about space on the Internet. On the Usborne Quicklinks Website there are links to four fun websites.

Website 1 -  Print out space pictures to fill in.

Website 2 -  Look at pictures of space food and guess what astronauts eat.

Website 3 -  Try all kinds of space games and activities.

Website 4 -  Dress up young astronauts and learn about parts of a spacesuit .

To visit these websites, go to **www.usborne-quicklinks.com** Read the Internet safety guidelines, and then type the keywords "beginners space".

The websites are regularly reviewed and the links in Usborne Quicklinks are updated. However, Usborne Publishing is not responsible, and does not accept liability, for the contect or availability of any website other than its own. We recommend that children are supervised while on the Internet.

# Index

airlock, 24, 30
bedroom, 15, 29
drink, 16-17, 22
Earth, 3, 4, 11, 12, 19, 21, 26, 28, 30
eating, 11, 15, 16-17, 29
exercise, 21, 29
food, 16-17
fuel tank, 6, 8, 9
gravity, 4, 30
jet pack, 24
laboratory, 20, 30
Moon, 17, 28

orbit, 10, 11, 30
parachute, 27
payload bay, 11, 25, 30
rockets, 6, 8, 9
shower, 15, 18
shuttle, 6, 7, 8, 9, 10, 11, 13, 14, 25, 26, 30
space station, 12-13, 14-15, 18, 20, 22, 24, 26, 30
spacesuits, 22-23, 24
spacewalking, 25
toilet, 15, 19
water, 5, 16, 18, 19, 23

## Acknowledgements

Cover design: Nicola Butler

**Photo credits**

The publishers are grateful to the following for permission to reproduce material:
© **Bristol Spaceplanes** 29, © **Corbis** (Richard T. Nowitz) 4, (Bettmann) 6, (Digital image © 1996 CORBIS; Original image courtesy of NASA/CORBIS) 9, (Bettmann) 16, (Roger Ressmeyer) 19, © **Digital Vision** Cover, 3, 26, © **Genesis Space Photo Library** 7, 19, © **NASA** Cover, 1, 5, 8, 12-13, 19, 20, 21, 23, 24, 25, 26-27, 28, 31

**With thanks to**
Katie Towers at Buxton Foods Ltd for the space strawberries.